2ND GRADE HISTORY:
THE MAYAN CIVILIZATION

SPEEDY
PUBLISHING

Speedy Publishing LLC
40 E. Main St. #1156
Newark, DE 19711
www.speedypublishing.com

The Maya civilization was a Mesoamerican civilization developed by the Maya peoples.

The Ancient Mayan lived in the Yucatán around 2000 B.C. This area is southern Mexico, Guatemala, northern Belize and western Honduras.

The Maya civilization is famous for its architecture. Many pyramids, temples, palaces and observatories are still standing today.

The Maya writing system was made up of 800 glyphs. Some of the glyphs were pictures and others represented sounds.

The Maya considered crossed eyes, flat foreheads, and big noses to be beautiful features. In some areas they would use makeup to try and make their noses appear large.

The Ancient
Maya developed
the science of
astronomy, calendar
systems and
hieroglyphic writing.

The Maya are perhaps most famous for their work in stone. Maya ceramics are an important art form.

Sometimes the ball games that the Maya played were part of a religious ceremony. The losers were sacrificed to the gods.

47691632R00020

Made in the USA
San Bernardino, CA
06 April 2017